HALLELUJAH
EVEN HERE

A Place for Your Grief to Breathe

MEREDITH P. NOLASCO

Published in the United States of America by
Spirit Media Publishing
Spirit Media and our logos are trademarks of
Spirit Media Inc
205 Academy Street STE 3251
Cary, NC 27519
1 (888) 800-3744 | www.spiritmediapublishing.com

Religion & Spirituality | Christian Books & Bibles | Spiritual Growth

Paperback ISBN: 979-8-89307-276-1
eBook ISBN: 979-8-89307-277-8
PDF ISBN: 979-8-89307-278-5
Library of Congress Control Number: 2026912421

For my husband, Hugo—
who stood beside me through this journey,
holding both love and grief,
carrying our family with a strength
shaped by his own scars.

Table of Contents

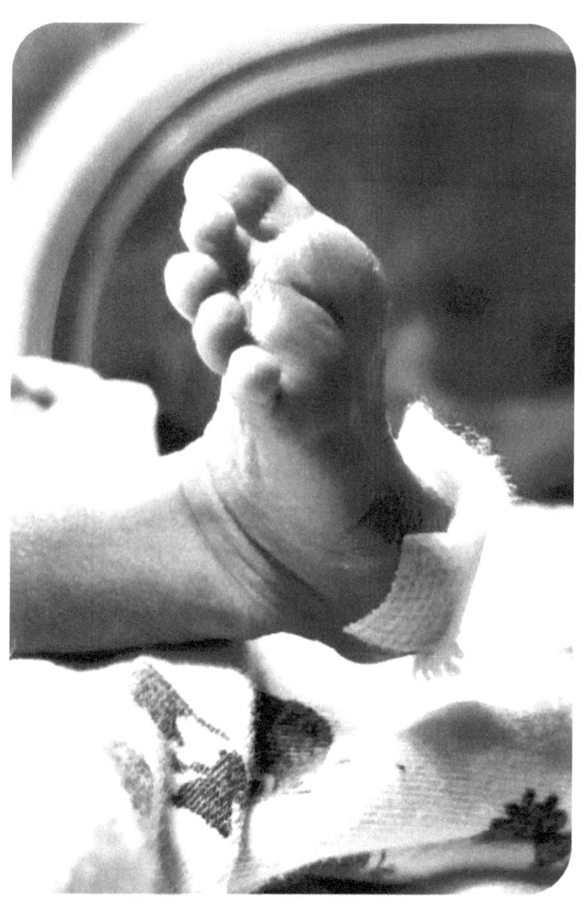

Carter Alexander Nolasco
(January 4 – January 16, 2026)

Introduction

I keep coming back to the same question: Why am I writing this?

Why do I feel compelled to put words to something that still feels impossible to hold? And every time, I land here—Because I have to.

There is a weight to Carter's story that will not let me stay silent. A sacred urgency that settles in my chest and does not lift until I let the words out.

God entrusted us with those two pounds, six ounces. A life that, by the world's standards, was brief—but in heaven's economy, was full of purpose. And somehow, that purpose now rests in the hands of his parents to carry and to share.

It feels like a burden. A holy one. The kind that wakes you in the morning and sits with you in the quiet. The kind that does not leave you alone until it is spoken.

So I write.

I write for the mothers who have known this kind of loss, who are searching for language for a pain that feels unspeakable.

I write for the fathers who stand beside them, holding a grief of their own while trying to steady the one they love.

I write for the babies whose stories seemed to end when their breath did, but whose lives were never without meaning. Each created on purpose, for a purpose.

And I write for myself, too. For the version of me that existed before Carter, untouched by this kind of sorrow. And for the version of me now, who knows, in a way I never wanted to learn, how fragile and miraculous life truly is.

But more than anything, I write for my son.

We never heard his cry. The world will never hear his voice. But they will hear his story.

And through it, they will see his Creator.

———

What this book is not…

This is not a guide on how to grieve.

It's not a roadmap, or a list of steps, or a promise that things will feel reconciled again if you just hold on long enough.

It's not a story that ties itself up neatly in the end.

I don't have answers for why a child dies. I don't have language that makes this make sense. And I won't try to force meaning into something that, this side of heaven, still aches.

This is also not a story without hope.

But the hope you'll find here isn't loud or easy. It doesn't erase sorrow or rush healing. It exists right alongside the pain… sometimes steady, sometimes barely there, but real.

This book is simply a telling.

Of our baby who lived. Of a mother who is still learning how to carry him. Of a God who meets us in places we never wanted to go.

CHAPTER 1

The Spring I Thought I Knew

We are planners.

As coaches, we walk with people through their health journey—systemizing where we can, optimizing as much as possible, and encouraging preparation. There is comfort in having a plan. In doing what you can ahead of time. In feeling ready.

Before Carter, I was a believer.

Not casually. Not culturally. My faith was personal—something I had chosen, even beyond the foundation I was raised in. I believed in God. I believed His Son Jesus died for my sins, and I trusted Him. I leaned on my faith in the places and to the extent I understood it. And still, I moved through life with a quiet confidence that things would work out.

I trusted God…and I trusted what I could control.

Even with a toddler—where a calm morning can turn into a full meltdown in seconds—we found a rhythm. Not perfect, but steady. Predictable enough to feel like we had some control. And as we prepared for Carter, that same rhythm carried us. Nothing rushed. Nothing chaotic. Just a quiet, intentional pace.

I took pride in doing things well. I stayed disciplined. I trained hard. I prioritized my health and paid attention to the details—nutrition, movement, appointments, timing.

We had experienced loss before—a miscarriage that had already shown us how fragile pregnancy can be. We knew things didn't always go as planned. We knew life wasn't guaranteed.

But there was still a quiet belief, subtle but steady, that if I showed up the right way, if I stewarded my body well, if I stayed consistent and aware…I could influence the outcome.

Not perfectly. But enough.

That's how I moved through pregnancy. Aware of the risks, but grounded in the belief that diligence mattered. That control, or at least influence, was mine to carry.

And I carried it well.

His name was chosen well before the world even knew I was pregnant.

Carter Alexander Nolasco. Perfect.

Carter's nursery was complete. Books filled his bookshelf, his crib was inviting, stuffed animals arranged, and I had just placed a new changing pad on his dresser. I could have waited to use Beckham's. But I didn't want everything to be passed down. I wanted Carter to have his own—his own space, his own start, his own place in our home.

His room was painted a beautiful shade of blue. Soft. Peaceful. Still. It's the most peaceful room in our house. It always has been.

Due in April, his nursery was prepared in December. We were ready. Or at least…we thought we were.

Because there is a kind of confidence that comes from preparation—a quiet belief that if you've done everything right, things will unfold the way they're supposed to.

My faith fit into that framework.

I trusted God, but I had never been brought to the place where trusting Him was all I had left. I had never had the ground fully give way beneath me. Not like this. If anything, my struggle in faith was never whether God was real—it was trying to understand why He would love me the way He does.

That kind of love always felt…undeserved. Hard to fully receive. Something I believed in theory, but didn't always know how to hold personally. But I had never questioned His goodness. Not deeply, and not in a way that cost me something.

You plan. You prepare. You create space.

And somewhere along the way, without saying it out loud, you begin to expect. Expect that the baby will come home. Expect that the room you built will be lived in. Expect that the life you are preparing for will arrive the way you imagined.

No one tells you how fragile that expectation is and how quickly it can unravel. How little control you actually have.

All the systems. All the preparation. All the readiness. And still, everything can change.

Not slowly, not with warning, but in a moment. The kind of moment that doesn't just interrupt your plans but exposes them. Because planning works until it doesn't. And when it doesn't, you're left standing in a room that was meant to hold life…trying to understand why it didn't.

When I look back, I wouldn't have changed our plans. I wouldn't have waited to prepare. I wouldn't have slowed down the love we poured into him before he ever arrived. But I would gently take my unscarred self by the shoulders and say, "Loosen your grip."

Cling more to God's sovereignty than to statistics and vague reassurances. Cling to His steadiness, not the probabilities of modern medicine. Hold tighter to the confident hope found in His presence—not in the outcome you're expecting. Because the truth is, every birth is an absolute miracle and holds Heavenly weight.

And all the plans in the world cannot stop His.

Ours didn't.

CHAPTER 2
Unraveling

It was a normal Sunday. We went to church that morning. Took Beckham for waffles after—the kind of slow, simple outing that feels like the rhythm of family life settling in. That afternoon we were in the backyard, kicking the soccer ball, letting him run and laugh.

Nothing about the day felt unusual. Nothing hinted at what was coming.

At some point, I started to feel discomfort, more than I had been feeling. Subtle at first. Easy to brush off. Maybe part of me didn't want to believe it was anything. So I kept going. Breathing through it. Telling myself it would pass.

But it didn't.

The pain sharpened. My body knew before my mind would catch up. And then everything accelerated.

One moment I was trying to steady myself—and the next, I was on the floor, shaking.

Hugo was on the phone with 911. And just like that, I was in labor.

What had been a normal Sunday unraveled in minutes. At twenty-seven weeks, my water broke and I was surrounded by firefighters and EMS.

Words started flying—ones I had never heard, but somehow immediately understood carried weight: Cord prolapse. Detached placenta.

And then the moment that changed everything—I couldn't feel my baby anymore.

No movement. No contractions. Just the silence of my womb...and the sound of sirens, deafening all the way to the hospital.

Everything felt urgent, but strangely still at the same time. Like my body and the world around me were moving fast, but internally I was frozen, trying to understand what was happening.

Then suddenly, contractions came back.

My body knew what to do—it was trying to get him out. But I wasn't allowed to push.

To save his life, a nurse had to physically hold him in, pushing back with everything she had. Holding him there. Buying time. Doing what felt impossible until the moment they could take me into surgery.

An emergency C-section. Bright lights. Voices moving quickly. My husband not allowed in the OR. I know he was frightened too.

I remember doctors yelling at each other through masks, "We don't have time—we have to get this baby out now!"

And then...a different kind of quiet.

Not peace. Not calm. The kind of silence that strips you of control and leaves you with nothing left to hold onto.

I whispered prayers through tears, asking God to go where I couldn't—into that room, into his tiny body, into an outcome I was no longer able to carry.

And then He was here.

Tiny. Fighting. Alive. A miracle I didn't earn, but received. And just like that, everything we had planned gave way to something we never would have chosen.

Our days became NICU monitors, quiet prayers, and learning how to parent in a space we never imagined. At the time, I didn't let my mind go anywhere else.

I never dreamed that Carter would not make it home from the NICU. It wasn't an outcome I entertained. Not even quietly.

Hope was there—steady, anchoring.

People reached out with stories. Babies born at twenty-four weeks. Twenty-five weeks. Now alive, thriving, and home.

I held onto those stories.

Not out of denial, but because they felt possible. Because they gave shape to a future I still believed we were walking toward.

And so even in the uncertainty…I expected him to come home.

CHAPTER 3
Eye of the Storm

The first time I walked to see him, I could feel every step.

Post-op, one hand pressed gently against my incision, one clutching my husband, my body weak and unsteady—but none of that seemed to matter. There was only one place I needed to be. With my baby.

The hallway felt longer than it should have. Slower than it should have. My body lagging behind what my heart was already reaching for.

And then I saw him. Our Carter.

So small. Bruised in ways I wasn't prepared for. Fragile, and yet, unmistakably fighting.

It was jarring and awe-inspiring all at once. The kind of moment where your mind tries to make sense of what your eyes are seeing, but can't quite catch up.

What a fighter.

All I wanted to do was sit there. Stay there. Be with him for as long as they would let me. But life was already pulling at me from two directions. A toddler at home. A newborn fighting for his life. It's a different kind of tearing that leaves a mother feeling like either way you love and you lose.

I was a mom to both.

The days quickly became filled with information—meetings with his care team, updates, numbers, terminology I didn't fully understand. I would nod along, trying to keep up, trying to grasp what mattered most. But even when I couldn't follow every detail, I could feel the weight of it.

Some meetings ended in tears. Some ended in silence. Most ended with the same question lingering in my mind—What do we do?

And underneath that...quieter, but heavier questions began to surface.

Why now? Why him? Why does an innocent life have to fight like this?

He was perfectly healthy in my womb. And now his lungs weren't ready for this world. I didn't have answers. And the ones I could have reached for felt too shallow for the weight of what we were living. My mind was going full speed all day long.

But I wasn't alone in the questions. Faith didn't remove them. If anything, it made me bring them somewhere. I found myself talking to God constantly—sometimes in steady prayers, sometimes in fractured sentences, sometimes in silence, just trusting He knew.

There were moments I felt undeniably held. Carried in a way I can't fully explain. And there were moments I wrestled.

Holding both at the same time—trust and confusion, peace and fear, hope and grief trying to creep in before its time. Somehow, both could exist.

And yet, there was a strange kind of peace in the NICU. Like the eye of a hurricane. A quiet that didn't feel empty, but sacred. Precious babies. Fragile lives. A stillness that made everything outside those walls feel distant. And honestly, it became the most peaceful part of my day. No distractions, no external noise, just me and my baby.

Hallelujah even here.

His little forehead would wrinkle when I spoke to him. He'd turn toward me when they removed his eye-shield. In all the unknowns of the world he entered, I had to believe he knew his mommy. I held onto those moments with everything in me because the space between his isolette and my arms felt impossible.

And somewhere in that space…in the quiet, in the questions, in the holding and the wrestling, I began to write.

Not as an author. Not even as someone trying to make sense of it all.

But as a mother, writing to her son.

January 8, 2026

Carter, you have arrived in a big way—unexpected, kind of scary, but here and fighting to claim the body God gave you and complete our family as only you can.

This is your NICU journey.

I may miss a few things and technical terms for all that is going on, but I want to hand you this one day as the earliest evidence of your fighting spirit and God's handwriting all over your story.

CHAPTER 4
Day 12

Day 12 of life.

That Friday started with a gift.

I wasn't expecting to hold my son. As I sat in the conference room with Carter's care team, the lead doctor looked at me and asked, "Would you like to hold him?" I can still see her smile.

I felt my heart leap. Yes. YES.

The cords, his fragility—it was all a big deal. It took an entire team of nurses and doctors to make it happen. But the moment we settled into the chair, with him resting on my chest, I felt my whole body exhale.

For a brief moment, all was well in our little corner of the world.

His hair was full and soft, his skin warm, and all I wanted to do was memorize him. His feet rested on my belly and his head on my chest. I nearly held my breath with each second, and yet wanted to escape in a deep inhale. It was the scent of my baby.

My baby.

One of the doctors instinctively grabbed my phone and began taking pictures. Those images would become a window into the most sacred hour of his time with us.

I imagine his little body recognized it—just softened into something familiar. Mommy. He was finally in the arms of his mommy. After fighting for twelve long days...he was held.

I didn't want to move. I watched the monitors, quietly tracking every number as they steadied.

The doctor smiled gently. "He is so happy."

Me too, I thought. Me too.

Before I left, I made plans with the nurse to come back in the morning—to spend the entire day with him. Now that I could hold my baby, I wanted to soak in every second as we counted down the days until he came home.

Until then, I would bring home to him.

———————————

I left that day still carrying the warmth of him on my chest.

It stayed with me. That deep exhale. That quiet confidence that maybe—we were turning a corner.

I went about the rest of my day holding onto it. Thinking about Saturday. Thinking about sitting with him for hours, uninterrupted. Letting myself imagine what it would feel like to just...be his mom without wires and teams and monitors between us.

I didn't know it would be the only time I would ever hold him full of life.

The first call came early that evening. One of the doctors. Calm, measured.

They were concerned. Carter's white blood cell count had risen and he was fighting an infection. They were waiting on more labs, but he had started declining that afternoon.

They were informing me. Staying ahead of it. I trusted them.

Okay, I thought. He's in good hands. They're on top of this.

The second call came not long after. The tone was different. They were preparing the surgical team—just in case this particular infection was confirmed. Still waiting on results.

My heart sank.

This was the first moment the thought broke through: He might not make it. And I didn't know what to do with that.

I couldn't be with him in surgery. I couldn't will him through it. I couldn't do anything and I had never felt so helpless.

Then the third call. No buffer. No easing in.

"How fast can you get here?"

"We've started chest compressions."

The ride to the hospital was a blur.

My hands trembled, my heart pounded, and tears were already streaming down my face. I knew what was coming, and yet preparing your heart for shattering is pointless. There is no preparation. You just let it shatter you.

I sprinted from the parking deck to the NICU. Twelve days after surgery, I clutched my incision, losing my breath in the cold January air. I had walked that same path earlier that day with anticipation, hope, and a steady heart. Now I ran in desperation.

The NICU doors were already open, as if they had prepared for my sprint. I turned the corner. Three nurses stood at the entrance of Pod G.

My heart sank again.

Was I too late? Oh God. I collapsed to the floor.

A nurse lifted me, steadying me as I sobbed, and guided me around the corner.

He was still alive.

The room was full, but I didn't see faces—just the blue of their uniforms and the weight hanging in the air that no one in that room wanted to carry.

The chair was already prepared for me, and they warned me he did not look the same. I winced. They gently transferred him into my arms, wrapped in his blanket, still tethered to tubes and cords.

Only hours before, I had sat there with his precious body on my chest, watching his heart and oxygen steady—taking in every second with hope. Now I sat cradling my baby, watching his heartbeat slow…as he slipped into eternity.

There were no words.

The beeps faded. They removed the tubes, escorted us to a private room, and gave us time.

Carter was gone.

My baby. My center of gravity. My reason for enduring the fear, the tears, the chaos of the NICU experience—gone.

How was it possible that his exit from the NICU was not in a car seat, heading home? Why was I holding his breathless body in my arms?

Why?

I felt lost. Unable to move.

We sat there for hours before finally making our way home.

Our world as we knew it was completely shattered.

CHAPTER 5
The Morning After

I woke up the next morning and for a brief second, everything felt normal.

There is a kind of mercy in that. A small, disoriented pause where your mind hasn't caught up yet.

Then it hit. Not gently. Not gradually. Like a wave that does not ask permission.

He's still dead.

I think I slept maybe thirty minutes that night. My head pounded. My body ached in a way I didn't know was possible. There were moments I was sure the weight of losing my son might actually kill me.

But I remember the silence. Long stretches of it, lingering in our house. We sat on the couch and just stared into nothing. If it hadn't been for a toddler running around, we could have gone the entire day without saying a word.

What was there to say?

Everything felt wrong. The light coming through the windows. The sound of the coffee machine. The ordinary rhythm of a morning that had no right continuing. How could the world move when mine had stopped?

I didn't even have the strength to ask God anything. The questions would come later—the wrestling, the searching, the "why?" But that day, I was too worn. Too emptied out to even reach for them.

Carter was gone. I was still his mom.

Both of those things existed at the same time, and I did not know what to do with that reality and ache. All I could do was sit in what was true…and somehow keep breathing.

In. Out. Again.

I knew God was there. He knew this moment was coming. And still, it felt like I was sitting in the aftermath of something that should never have been allowed.

February 9, 2026

My first post-surgery/birth appointment today just brought more tears and no answers. Having to say "my son passed away in the NICU" rips me open every single time. I break down and want to just crawl in a hole.

I'm numb to hearing "I'm so sorry for your loss" that I often don't respond. I don't know what to say to that anymore.

The doctors had no answers as to why the abruption happened. None. Everything was healthy. No infection. No trauma. No reason as to why labor started and immediately put my baby in danger.

Carter was healthy and well until forced into this world and facing dangers he never faced in my womb. And I couldn't protect him.

My heart breaks all over again.

Surrendering my desire for answers feels like a repeated, daily step. I lay it at His feet and in a moment of desperation and panic, I go to pick it back up.

I know better, and yet I do.

My humanity is weak. As if knowing would ease the pain or make it make sense. But nothing…No explanation. No signs. No warning. All healthy.

Just here—and then gone.

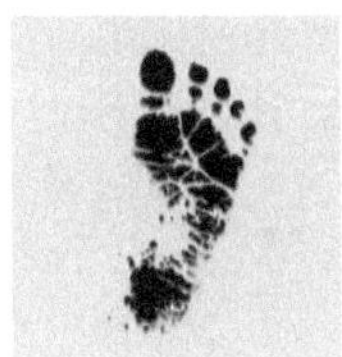

CHAPTER 6
Shock Is a Mercy

Every moment of the NICU felt surreal. The room hummed with the steady rhythm of monitors and ventilators—a quiet, mechanical soundtrack to the most fragile days of our lives. We went from anticipating three more months of pregnancy to completely reorienting around Carter almost overnight.

He became our center of gravity.

Every day, Hugo and I coordinated schedules between clients and childcare just to make it to the hospital. Life outside those walls still existed—emails, responsibilities, people who needed us—but everything bent toward the same destination.

Toward Carter.

We would sit with him, talk to him, pray over him.

The small door on the side of the isolette became my gateway to my son.

"Hey baby, it's mommy," I would whisper each time I slipped my hand through the opening.

Almost without fail, his tiny forehead would wrinkle in response, like he recognized the voice that had carried him for months.

I know he knew.

When doubt tries to creep in—when the quiet questions of grief begin whispering—I return to those moments. The warmth of his skin beneath my hand. The subtle movements that told me my son knew I was there.

For twelve days, our lives rearranged themselves around that rhythm.

And then suddenly, it was over.

Going from a life that had so drastically adjusted to his presence…to "no more"…was a shock my mind and body struggled to comprehend.

I felt disoriented.

With time.

With conversations.

With the strange reality of a world that kept moving.

Inside, everything in me had been dismantled. Shock is a strange mercy.

It steps in when the full weight would crush you. It softens reality just enough for you to function.

You answer texts. You make decisions. You thank people for meals. You carry on small conversations.

But the truth sits just outside of you—not fully felt yet.

I knew the words. I could say them if I had to.

"Our son died."

But the sentence felt distant, like it belonged to someone else's story.

Shock held the line for a while.

It allowed me to stand when my legs should have given out. Memories of Carter's traumatic birth existed, but they felt far away. My mind wasn't there yet.

Instead, it stayed fixed on one simple, incomprehensible reality:

Our son was gone.

Time felt distorted. Conversations drifted past me. I could hear people talking, but it felt like I was standing just outside my own life, watching it unfold. Shock protected me.

But it is not permanent.

Eventually, it loosens its grip. And when it does, sorrow begins to seep in through the cracks.

Not all at once—just enough at first to let you know it's there.

The silence in the house feels louder than it should. There are no more drives to the hospital. No more slipping my hand through the isolette door. No more whispering, "Hey baby, it's mommy."

That is when sorrow settles in—not as something distant, but as something that lives inside your chest.

Shock protected me. Sorrow exposed me.

Shock said, "This can't be real." Sorrow says, "It is."

At first, grief anchors itself in the absence—the empty space where your child should be. The quiet house. The missing weight in your arms. The future that suddenly disappears. But eventually, the mind begins to wander backward.

The memories come quietly. A flicker you can't quite hold onto. A sound. A sentence. The image of fluorescent lights passing overhead as they rushed me down the hallway.

Then they begin to stay.

The ambulance ride. The stillness in my womb. The unspoken anticipation of words no parent is ready to hear.

I didn't realize at the time that I was carrying two different weights: The grief of losing my son. The trauma of how he entered the world.

As those memories slowly returned, I began to see something else I had not noticed in the moment…God's quiet mercy inside the shock.

Scripture speaks of God as our refuge—our shelter, our hiding place.

Shock, in its own strange way, felt like that shelter.

The Lord did not ask my heart to carry the full weight of Carter's story all at once. He gave it to me in pieces—small enough to hold.

Because He knows what we are made of.

He remembers that we are dust.

Looking back, I can see the kindness in that.

Because if every moment had landed at once—the fear in the ambulance, the chaos of the hospital, the fragile days in the NICU, and then the moment we had to say goodbye—I don't know that my heart could have held it.

But He did.

Even when my mind could not yet look at it and when my heart was still trying to understand.

And slowly—very slowly—He began to walk me back through it.

CHAPTER 7
Two Strands

Scripture repeatedly tells us that God is near to the broken-hearted—the grieving, those caught in the depths of sorrow. From the moment Carter went to be with Jesus, I have experienced that for myself.

There is a kind of pain that has no words. And somehow, there is also a comfort that has no words.

It is beyond anything I can fully comprehend—that in the middle of tragedy, a person can feel held. Held by the same God who parted the Red Sea, who created the heavens and the earth, who knew you before you were formed in the womb.

It's a different kind of hold.

Not God in the burning bush, or the thunder, but God in the silence.

I think He knows the circumstance and the pain are loud enough. What I have needed most is not more noise, but the ability to hear my own breath—to find oxygen again in the quiet.

He meets me where I am. And He continues to orchestrate moments that only He could.

One day I was looking at a picture of Carter, as I often do. The first thing I always notice is his hair—even at just twenty-seven weeks it was full, soft, absolutely beautiful. And I had the thought, I should have kept a small piece of it.

Naturally, I find myself clinging to anything that validates his short existence here with us.

Only a few days later, I sat in his room like I do most afternoons, his ashes held close to my chest, his hospital blanket in my lap. I often peel back the layers—still stained in places—and bring it to my nose, searching for one more trace of my baby.

It's wild how primal that is. To smell your child, and for a moment, feel grounded…almost euphoric. The scent is virtually gone now. But I still search.

This time, as I pulled back another layer, there they were—two small pieces of his hair, intertwined, caught in the fabric.

They must have been there since the day he lay swaddled at the funeral home.

God knew I would need that moment. He knows every hair on Carter's head…and He left a couple for his mom.

Something for my love to touch. Something to witness when the weight of the loss feels like too much. And maybe that's what His sovereignty looks like up close.

Not just in the grand, unsearchable plans we wrestle to understand, but in the smallest, most intimate details we didn't even know to ask for.

A God who governs the galaxies…and also tucks two strands of hair into a blanket, knowing the exact day a grieving mother would find them. A God who is not distant from our pain, but attentive to it. Intentional within it.

He does not waste moments. He does not overlook the details. He does not forget His children.

I don't audibly hear God's voice. But He makes His presence known in the details.

I see Him—because He sees me.

CHAPTER 8
"I Can't Imagine"

"I can't imagine."

When people say this, I don't hear distance anymore. I hear truth. They can't.

Not because this kind of loss is unreachable, but because God gives us our daily bread. Personal. Specific. For the moment we're breathing in and navigating through.

My daily bread right now includes the strength and mercy to carry the death of my child. Theirs does not.

And if our stories were different, the bread would be too.

There are days I wake up and think, I can't do this. And in a way, that's still true. I can't do all of it. I can't carry the full weight of this loss in one breath, one thought, one lifetime.

But I'm not asked to.

I'm given just enough for today. My manna.

Enough grace to get out of bed. Enough strength to take the next step. Enough mercy to hold both the sorrow and the love without collapsing under it.

So when someone says, "I can't imagine," it's true. They can't.

Because imagination isn't what sustains you here. Daily bread is.

CHAPTER 9
Friday

Every day feels like Friday.

I wish I meant that in the light, easy way—like the world is winding down, like there's something to look forward to just around the corner. A break. A breath. But I don't.

Friday is the day I said goodbye to my sweet Carter.

So when my eyes open each morning and my feet hit the floor, before I'm even fully awake, my mind goes to him. His face. The weight of him. The way his little forehead would wrinkle when I spoke.

And then the second thought comes, just as quickly, just as sharp—He's still dead.

There's no gentle way to say it. I've tried to soften it, to dress it up in words that feel easier to carry. But "passed away" doesn't hold the weight of it. It doesn't land the way it actually lands in my chest each morning.

So I don't soften it.

Because this is the reality I wake up to, whether I want to or not.

It hits like a sucker punch. Not because I've forgotten. I haven't, not for a second. But because there's this tiny, fleeting moment when I first wake up where life feels untouched. Almost normal. And then it rushes back in.

Oh...right. This is real. This is my life.

Over and over again.

Friday.

It's strange how grief marks time. It doesn't move forward in clean lines the way the calendar says it should. It loops. It returns. It anchors itself to a moment and keeps bringing you back there, whether it's been days or months or years.

And layered on top of that is the timeline my body remembers—pregnancy, anticipation, milestones, heartbeats, the expectation of delivery.

And now I sit here trying to comprehend that in a matter of weeks, I have delivered, fed, held, hoped, said goodbye...and watched my body return to a pre-pregnancy state—all just days shy of his due date.

My mind can't fully hold it.

Friday. Not just once a week—every day.

And yet...the day still moves.

Emails still need answering. Beckham still laughs. Life still asks something—no, everything—of me.

And there's this quiet tension I carry—living in a world that keeps moving forward, while part of me is still standing in Friday, January 16th, holding my son and not wanting to let go. I'm still his mom.

I don't know that this ever fully goes away.

And somehow, by the grace of God, I get up anyway.

The to-do list still sits in front of me—ordinary things, the kind of things that used to feel automatic in the rhythm we had before Carter.

Running a business. Laundry. Dishes. Toy cleanup. Books to read. A toddler to chase.

I remember in the days right after Carter passed, I wanted to scream. I wanted to burn the laundry, let the dishes pile up, and collapse on the floor. None of it mattered. Or at least that's what I thought.

I thought I had reached the deepest kind of apathy imaginable.

But it wasn't apathy. It was perspective.

My soul had tasted eternity.

Scripture tells us in Ecclesiastes that life under the sun is vapor—fleeting. And Carter's last breath forced me to feel that in my bones, not just understand it in my mind.

Everything that once felt urgent...suddenly wasn't.

But that doesn't mean it's meaningless. The ordinary still matters—because love is still there. I care for our home because God has given us a place to land, a haven to hold both grief and joy at the same time.

I wash clothes because what a gift it is to dress our son, to watch Beckham run around in his favorite color, blue.

I respond to clients because God, in His kindness, has given us work that serves people and uses the gifts He placed in us.

Right now, while my capacity is low, the ordinary is God's mercy. It's enough and it matters. Not because it's grand, but because it's faithful. It's perspective colliding with responsibility. And in that tension, God's love meets me—not in fireworks, but in foundation. Steady. Unmoving.

Somehow, He still brings morning.

February 21, 2026

My head is pounding this morning. I've gotten used to the fatigue, but the migraines from crying always feel jarring.

Seeing a counselor yesterday was beneficial overall, but recounting the story stirs the questions in my mind once more and I find myself going down the rabbit hole of what-ifs, trying to create order out of chaos.

I hear "You're processing this in a healthy way"—but what does that actually mean?! I'm constantly falling apart.

I don't feel hopeless, but life is so gray and nothing sounds appealing to me. I just want to feel my baby near. I want to remember him in warmth, in light, in those precious minutes where our little slice of the world seemed to stand still.

That's what I crave.

CHAPTER 10
Ashes

The question caught me off guard. "Was it a hard decision to cremate him?"

I answered quickly. Too quickly, almost.

"No."

And even as the word left my mouth, I felt a flicker of surprise at how certain it sounded. Not rehearsed. Not wrestled through. Just…settled.

Because when I thought about Carter, I didn't think in abstract terms. I thought about the boy I knew. Even in the NICU, he didn't like being confined.

He would stretch his legs out, pressing against the boundaries around him, like his little body was always reaching for more space. And something in me couldn't bear the thought of him being placed underground. Still. Enclosed. Distant.

It made my chest tighten.

So the decision didn't feel like a decision at all. It felt like recognition.

There is a kind of irony, I guess. He is now in a box. Sitting in his crib. But he is close.

And sometimes I take the bag of his ashes out, hold them against my chest, and just breathe. Everything in me slows. My mind quiets. For a moment, it feels like harmony.

I know his soul is not there. I know where he is. But love still reaches for what it can touch.

And maybe that's what this was.

Part of it is me—a mother wanting her son near. But part of it feels like I knew him. Not fully. Not in the way I was supposed to over years and birthdays and daily rhythm in our home. But enough.

Enough to recognize what felt right for him. Enough to answer without hesitation. And maybe that's one of the quiet mercies God gives—that even in twelve days, a mother can know her child.

CHAPTER 11
When the Body Still Remembers

I dove headfirst into many books after Carter went to be with Jesus. I wanted to hear from parents who navigated this dark valley, who spoke to their humanity, carried hope, and perhaps some insight into the question that lingers in your soul when your child is no longer earth side:

What now?

My heart ached with them. Every account just makes you long for eternity in ways you never thought possible. You hear them, you grieve with them, you see them.

It's a fraternity that too many are a part of, and the initiation one that no one would ever choose. I clung to their words, but I found myself stuck. What about all the behind-the-scenes a mother has to face just after her baby passes?

My milk came in. My scar still healing. My body in a panic because while my mind knows my baby is gone, my body does not.

It kept doing what it was designed to do.

Providing. Longing. Mothering.

It took me close to two months for my milk to dry up, and the process was incredibly painful. For the first couple of weeks following his passing, I'd wake up in the middle of the night to pump. In the dark, headphones on, and just sobbing.

Those moments were dark. A loneliness that does not leave out of will, but you simply lean into because what choice do you have until biology catches up?

The hospital could not take my supply.

I'll never forget calling the NICU the morning after Carter died. My hands were trembling. I hadn't slept. I was disoriented from shock. I finally managed to say:

"Hi...my son passed away last night. Could I bring you my milk for the other babies?"

It took me what felt like a full minute just to get that sentence out. She kindly explained why they couldn't take it. I said, "Okay, thank you."

Hung up the phone. And just groaned. That deep cry that echoes in your bones.

For weeks I watched my body long for my baby, produce food, and then pour it down the drain. Like my love had nowhere to land and my body had no one to feed.

I know God wastes nothing. But every ounce I discarded was salt on a hemorrhaging wound.

I pumped. I poured. I cried. I thanked God for that. My body was doing what it was designed to do. Grief and gratitude. Holding both will stretch your soul further than you can imagine.

I remember when it finally stopped. It was the day before Beckham's second birthday, and it was another moment when life and grief collided head on, full speed. Another physical thread tying me to my Carter on this side of eternity was coming to a close.

Part of me was relieved to no longer have the constant physical reminder of loss. The other part of me was clinging to anything that still connected me to my baby. Truth is, there is a twinge of guilt in feeling both. Grief is messy.

But God showed me something powerful in this: My milk was a sign of connection, but it was never the source of it.

Feel the pain. Feel the guilt. Feel the loss. Feel the gratitude. Then lay all of it at His feet.

I confess, before Carter I found it easy to forget that Jesus is also "A Man of sorrows and acquainted with grief" (Isaiah 53:3 NKJV). In short, He gets it. He lived it. He covers us as we walk through it.

So why would I hold onto such heavy sorrow and pain that was not mine to carry alone? I couldn't carry it. Many days I thought it would kill me.

I had to lay it down.

———————————

Meanwhile, my body started to return to "pre-baby" rhythms. Quietly signaling life moving forward while my heart was still anchored to the child who should be here.

Ovulation is such a biological, matter-of-fact thing. Your body just does it. There's no ceremony, no acknowledgment of what you've been through. And so when you notice it, it can feel like your body is saying, *We're ready to start again.*

While your heart screams, *But I'm not finished loving the one I just had.*

Biology is beautiful, and brutal. There isn't a tidy theological explanation to place neatly over that tension.

But in my longing for Carter, God also sees the need for healing and space for life. He does not rush the emotional side of things. But like a loving Father does, He quietly tends to the things behind the scenes.

Immersed in grief, I never asked for my ovaries to wake back up. But He made sure they did.

It was His original, holy design anyway. I didn't have to ask.

He knew.

March 13, 2026

In my most honest moments, I don't want my body to be returning to "my old self." I want to be nine months pregnant. That old self is gone. Somewhere between the sprint to the NICU and carrying his lifeless body out of Pod G, that woman died too.

CHAPTER 12
Brothers

Raising Beckham while grieving Carter is a constant tension of being pulled into the present while aching for what is no longer here. Beckham brings a joy that anchors me. He pulls me into the now—into laughter, into play, into the small, ordinary moments that still exist. He is a gift. A steady, living reminder that life is still moving, still unfolding right in front of me.

And at the very same time…he is also a reminder of Carter's absence. That's just the unfiltered reality. There is no clean separation between the two. Joy and grief don't take turns. They don't politely give each other space. They stand side by side. Like brothers.

One pulling me into laughter, the other into longing. Both belonging to me and shaping me at the same time.

Beckham keeps me busy, which in many ways is a mercy. But grief is not something that disappears just because your hands are full. It waits. It lingers. It asks for its own space. And I've learned I have to be intentional about giving it that space. Because a grieving mother needs somewhere to go with her sorrow.

What has surprised me is not the joy. I haven't felt overwhelming guilt for laughing or feeling moments of lightness the way some people describe. I've received those moments for what they are: gifts. God provides those moments in perfect timing.

But I do feel guilt in other places. I feel it when I cry in front of Beckham.

It often happens at night, when the day has worn me down. We're sitting together, reading bedtime stories, turning pages filled with little animals and soft rhymes. And suddenly, the weight hits.

"Why is Mommy crying?"

At two years old, he is observant and leans into my feelings more often than I'd prefer. So there is a pause. A sigh. And then I answer his question with simplicity that he understands and gravity that feels too heavy for three words.

"Mommy misses Carter."

I realize I will never sit here with Carter. I will never read him these books. Never smell the baby shampoo in his hair. Never rock him and sing him to sleep. And the tears come before I can stop them. In those moments, I feel like I'm failing Beckham.

I am supposed to protect him, to preserve his innocence. To shield him from the weight of a broken world for as long as I can. And yet here I am, with a tear-soaked face, letting him see a sorrow I pray he never has to carry on this side of eternity.

There's a helplessness in that. But there is also a truth I am slowly learning to hold: He is not only seeing my sorrow. He is seeing love.

He is seeing what it looks like to love someone so deeply that their absence is felt, not just spoken. He is seeing that our family holds both joy and grief, and that neither one pushes the other out.

And maybe, in some quiet way, that is forming something in him too.

Right now, mothering both of my sons takes everything in me. Loving Beckham with presence and patience. Loving Carter with memory and longing. Holding one in my arms, while carrying the other in my heart.

And somewhere in the middle of all of this…God is present.

Not removing the tension. Not asking me to choose joy over grief or grief over joy. But steady within it. A Father who understands what it is to love a Son. A God who does not waste love, or loss, or the aching space in between.

I don't always understand how to move in this space, this tension, this part of our story that constantly feels unresolved. But I do trust that He is in it with me. That He sees both of my boys. That He holds Carter in eternity and walks with me as I love Beckham here. And that somehow, in ways I cannot yet see, He is sustaining me to be a mother to both.

CHAPTER 13
Mothering on Both Sides

I always loved the thought of having my sons in the spring.

Celebrating Beckham in March and then Carter in April. Something about it felt like a fresh start to the season—new life, longer days…and if I'm honest, maybe even combined birthday parties.

When I look back on those dreams, I mourn for that version of me.

Not innocent by any means—but untouched by this kind of loss. Not yet shaped by death or the weight of grief that rewrites you from the inside out.

Planning Beckham's birthday in the days and weeks after Carter passed required a strength that was not my own. He deserved every bit of joy. Every laugh. Every unfiltered, light-filled moment.

And he had them. But my heart ached the entire time.

Thank God for the close friends who showed up—who could celebrate Beckham while also holding space for me as I slipped into tears or a quick memory about Carter.

My brain is all over the place these days—going from "where are the candles?" to "let me tell you about Carter's hair" feels like mental ping-pong.

And it's a game I can only play with a handful of really beautiful souls.

Some people want distraction from grief. I don't.

There's no right or wrong in that—but for me, stepping away from it only makes the return more violent. The emotional whiplash is worse than learning how to carry it in real time. So I stay close. Even when I'm planning a party. Even when I'm tying balloons and cutting cake.

Grief doesn't pause for celebration. It just learns to sit beside it.

It's grief colliding with responsibility. And it's messy.

I'm still mothering a child on this side of eternity. And sometimes that means the balloons and birthday candles exist in the same space as sorrow.

It feels unfair. But it's real life.

And I think about David. After he lost his son, Scripture says he got up. He washed his face. He ate. Not because the grief was gone—but because life, somehow, was still moving.

I understand that now in a way I never could before. You rise, not because you're okay—but because something in you is being held by God in ways you can't explain. Rising doesn't mean healed. It means sustained.

After the weekend of celebrating, I go into Carter's room. And it feels like I can finally lay it all down. The armor comes off. I exhale.

It's like centering myself again. No performing. No hosting. No holding the emotional weight of the room. Just me, my son, and my Savior.

That space is sacred to me. It holds both peace and pain—the peace of closeness, and the ache of longing.

My heart orients toward Carter there. I mother him in that room.

There is a steadiness in it.

My body and my heart finally stop bracing. Grief keeps everything on high alert—the replaying, the ache, the noise of the world pressing in. But when I sit there, holding his ashes, something inside me settles. This is where my love for him rests and everything quiets.

That stillness doesn't take the grief away. It just gives it somewhere to breathe.

I don't have this figured out. But I know this: God is meeting me in both places.

In the noise of celebration and in the silence of Carter's room. In the strength it takes to stand up and in the surrender it takes to fall apart.

And maybe that's what this season is teaching me. Not how to move on, but how to carry both. To celebrate the life in front of me while still aching for the life I can't hold.

This is motherhood now. On both sides of eternity.

February 28, 2026

I'm learning that gratitude and grief can sit in the same breath. I can feel the sun on my face and still ache for the weight lying on my chest. I can be thankful for this life—for mornings, for love, for the people still here— and still miss you so fiercely it steals the air from my lungs.

It isn't one or the other. It's both.

A heart split wide open, holding beauty in one hand and loss in the other, somehow carrying them together.

CHAPTER 14
Constant Collision

Grief intrudes on life. Life intrudes on grief. Repeat.

It's being in tears when a flashback hits, while your toddler is tugging at your sleeve, needing you now.

It's shopping for a birthday party while receiving a text about your other son's memorial service.

It's the dress for the memorial arriving in the middle of the birthday celebration.

It's savoring a quiet moment to remember him, only for your phone to buzz with business demands.

It's crying and still having to show up. It's showing up and leaving in tears.

Wave upon wave.

This is the strange rhythm of grief: sorrow and life, colliding again and again.

It's been over two months since Carter passed, and while I can navigate conversations about him, and even smile in the remembrance, there are still moments that completely shatter me.

A local cashier I haven't seen in months asks, "How old is the baby now?"

Shatter.

Will I ever get used to saying, "my son passed away," without completely breaking apart in the moment?

Maybe that day will come. But not yet.

And maybe...that's not something I'm meant to rush.

It's often my mind reminding my heart that grief isn't something to solve. It's something to carry. Not all at once, but as it comes.

And there is a surrender here I'm still learning. It's not always instinctual. That surrender is a posture. A choice. Because it's not surrender in the sense of giving up, but in loosening my grip on how I think this should look.

Letting the waves come without bracing so hard against them. Letting joy exist without questioning it. Letting sorrow come without trying to contain it.

Maybe rhythm isn't something you find in grief. Maybe it's something you yield to.

A rhythm that doesn't ask permission. That doesn't follow logic. That doesn't resolve neatly. But somehow...through grace, it carries you anyway.

January 27, 2026

Honoring grief while raising a toddler is a quiet kind of tearing.

Grief asks for stillness. Toddlers ask for presence, movement, immediacy. One wants silence. The other wants me, right now.

Some days I feel torn between being "on" for Beckham and longing to quietly grieve Carter. Between snacks and stories and diapers...and the ache to sit in the stillness and be with my son who cannot cry out for my touch.

It's showing up for the child in front of me, and giving presence to the child still very much with me. Love doesn't divide neatly. It stretches. It overlaps. It hurts.

I'm learning that honoring grief doesn't require constant attention—it waits. Stillness can be small. Steady. Love finds its way in fragments. It doesn't ask us to choose between love and loss—it asks us to learn how to hold both. To make room, in the ordinary, noisy, beautiful days.

CHAPTER 15

April 5th

I remember seeing the date, April 5th. In my mind, that day would make me a mother of another precious baby boy.

You cling to a future date that suddenly alters your perspective on that season, that month, and that day. Everything begins to organize itself around it. What life will look like then. Who you will be when it arrives and suddenly two more feet enter your home.

Now, as I sit writing this, we are just days away from his due date and there is no pregnant belly. No swollen feet. No hospital bag by the door. No quiet anticipation building in our home.

Instead, I am planning his memorial.

As I write this, I should be 39 weeks pregnant. The threshold weeks. The "any day now." The hospital bag by the door. The countdown.

Instead, I'm living in two realities at once.

In one, I'm pregnant. Tracking kicks. Measuring time in weeks. In the other, he's here. He was here. He's gone.

It's a shock my body keeps having to relearn.

I thought the one-month mark of his death would be painful. It was. But not like this.

My mind still does the math—Pregnant. Not pregnant. He's almost here. He lived. He died.

Grief is disorienting like that. It doesn't just take a person, it takes the timeline you were walking toward. It leaves you standing in the "almost there" space with no place to arrive.

Most days it feels like love is trying to find footing in a story that changed without permission.

I remember each appointment, the nurse smiling as she said, "He's measuring right on time, to the day." Not early. Not late. Right on time.

And now I can't escape the tension that sits between what I was told and what has unfolded. By earthly standards, he arrived thirteen weeks early. Extreme prematurity. A timeline interrupted and a story cut short.

But by God's sovereignty…he was not early. He arrived as planned.

And sometimes I don't know what to do with that.

Because if he was "on time" in the eyes of a sovereign God, then this was not a disruption. This was not an accident. This was not something that slipped through His hands.

Which means the date I circled in hope, April 5th, was never the day I would bring him home.

My humanity wrestles with that.

Because everything in me still aches for the version of this story where I am counting kicks, timing contractions, packing tiny clothes into a hospital bag. Instead, I am counting days since I last held him.

I am choosing a dress for his memorial instead of an outfit for his arrival.

I am preparing to honor a life when I thought I would be welcoming one.

Two timelines. One I lived in expectation. One I now live in reality.

And somewhere in the middle of that tension is God. Not explaining it. Not softening it. Not asking me to pretend it makes sense.

Just here. Sovereign over the days I thought I would have and the twelve I was given.

Yes, I am still learning what it means to trust Him in a story that does not follow the timeline I believed was good. And yet, even this date—the one I thought I understood—is not untouched by His hand.

April 5th falls on Easter Sunday.

What a God-ordained convergence, to hold two very real truths at the same time: Death is real. And His love is greater than death.

Our home never heard his newborn wail, but Heaven certainly did.

And Carter's life, though painfully short, is woven into the greatest promise of our faith: that Jesus conquered death, and what feels final here is not final in eternity.

So this Easter will feel different.

It will carry the ache of an empty crib, and the steady, anchoring hope found in an empty tomb.

Our grief is real. Our longing is real. But so is the promise that death does not win.

And somehow, in a way only God could write, Carter's story rests right in the middle of that truth…quietly pointing us back to his Creator.

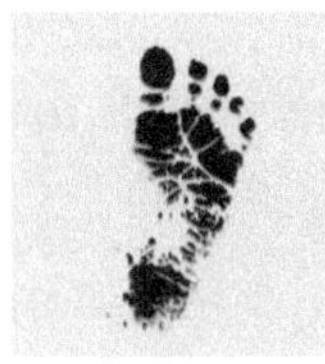

CHAPTER 16
"How Are You Doing?"

I don't know that there can be a more complicated question to answer after losing a child. In many ways, the answer seems obvious.

Not good. Not okay. Barely standing. Often falling apart.

Those are the answers that remain true most of the time.

And yet, if you asked anyone this question in the wake of that kind of loss, I'd be willing to bet the answer you receive is a filtered one. Not because they intentionally want to hand you platitudes, but because there is a strange discomfort hanging in the air. An unspoken tension.

Because in some ironic way, we are now managing the emotions of the very person asking about ours.

Can they handle the honest answer? What if I told them I wept on the floor until I couldn't breathe? That sometimes I scream. That when someone complains about something trivial, everything inside of me wants to shout, I don't care.

And truth is, both answers—the filtered one and the tap-water honest one—are exhausting. You simply learn who has the emotional capacity to hold space for your sorrow and who does not.

It is no fault of their own. It's just human.

You make a quiet mental note. You protect the tender places of your heart. And at the same time, you feel deep gratitude for the few who are willing to walk further into the garden with you.

Even Jesus only had a few. He didn't call all His disciples into Gethsemane with Him to pray and weep. He knew something we eventually learn through suffering.

He took three.

So perhaps it shouldn't surprise us that most people, even kind, well-intentioned ones, will not go in the garden with you.

And maybe that's more than okay. But it also means you find yourself standing there…with very few.

CHAPTER 17
Why a Child?

The conversations end. The room quiets. And what remains are the questions no one knows how to ask.

Why a child?

Adult eulogies usually recount a life that had time to unfold.

They tell stories of accomplishments, personality, milestones—the things someone built, contributed, or became over decades. But when a child dies, those categories disappear.

There are no career milestones. No long list of stories. No years of memories for the world to observe.

And so the question presses harder: Why a child?

Because when a life is measured in days instead of decades, the usual ways we make sense of it simply don't work anymore.

Carter's eulogy could not point to accomplishments. It could not recount a life built over time. At most, it could describe a fragile fight for life that began at just twenty-seven weeks.

And as Hugo worked through what to say, I remember thinking: There is nothing earthly to point to here.

And maybe…that is the story.

Because when everything else is stripped away, it leaves only one direction for your eyes to go: Up.

That question—why a child—became deeply personal before Carter ever passed.

When my water broke at home, everything turned chaotic. Paramedics filled our house. I was in labor, but Carter was not positioned safely, and the situation escalated quickly.

And then, suddenly—the contractions stopped. Completely.

———————

On the way to the hospital, my body was quiet. And in that silence, my mind began bracing for the words no parent is prepared to hear:

"We're so sorry…"

But the moment we entered the hospital, everything changed. The contractions returned. Carter was alive.

And that moment has never left me. Because it raises a question I still carry:

God, why would You save him…only to take him twelve days later?

Why bring him through that moment? Why give him strength to survive birth, only for us to lose him anyway? Why let us meet him, hold him, love him…just to say goodbye?

It is a question that echoes. And sometimes, it aches.

———————

Scripture is honest about something we struggle to accept: God does not promise that we will understand the why behind suffering.

Job is never given an explanation. David laments without resolution. Even Jesus wept at Lazarus' tomb, knowing resurrection was moments away.

God does not rebuke the ache, but He rarely explains. What Scripture does show us is something different: That every life, long or short, exists to glorify Him.

We tend to measure purpose by years. By accomplishments. By visible impact. But the Bible dismantles that. Sometimes a life becomes a window through which the works of God are displayed.

Displayed. Not always explained.

Carter's life was only twelve days long. And yet, those twelve days have drawn people to prayer. They have awakened eternal perspective. They have softened hearts and reminded us how fragile and sacred life truly is. His story has pointed people to God.

No human accomplishments to list, but a greater eternal purpose completed. To glorify his Creator.

This does not remove the ache.

I write this in the light of his room with his ashes to my chest, still very aware of a longing that will never leave on this side of eternity. We wish Carter were here. We wish we were watching him grow, hearing his cry, holding him in the middle of the night. We would choose that every time. But his life reminds us that purpose is not measured by length of days. Only by the fact that he was here at all. Created on purpose. For a purpose.

So no—Carter's life isn't something that fits into the way we usually define a life. There are no decades to recount. No list of accolades. But there was a heartbeat. There was breath. If the purpose of life is to point to the glory of God—then his life did exactly that. And I imagine my baby heard "well done" (Matthew 25:21 NIV) as he entered eternity.

We may never understand why his story was written this way.

But we do know this: His life was complete and his testimony is not over. The same God who formed him, sustained him, and carried him home is the God who promises resurrection. And because of Jesus, death does not get the final word.

So we grieve, but we do not grieve without hope. Because one day, we will see our son again. Not fragile. Not fighting. Not surrounded by machines.

Whole. Alive. Home.

Until then, Carter's existence and echo will continue to do what they have already begun to do—point us, and everyone who hears his story, to his Heavenly Father.

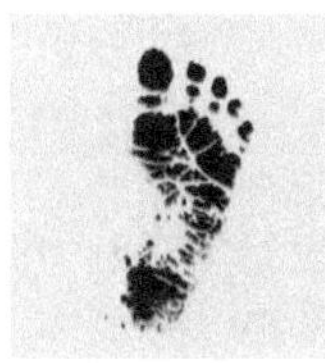

CHAPTER 18
Fragile, But Not Broken

I can understand now how this kind of loss breaks a marriage.

The sorrow is relentless. The grief is exhausting. And it asks two flawed human beings to somehow navigate the unimaginable, hand in hand.

Hugo and I are grieving the same loss...but from different vantage points. We grieve differently. We carry our son differently. There are moments I don't understand him. And moments he doesn't understand me. He has continued to pour himself into providing for our family, steady and unwavering. He shows up for me in ways I didn't know how to ask for—supporting my grief, making space for it, even when he can't fully make sense of it.

He doesn't always understand why I sometimes choose to stay close to the wound. But he honors it, and loves me where I am. And I am deeply aware, that is a gift.

I didn't understand, at first, why he couldn't spend much time in Carter's nursery...when all I wanted to do was curl up in the crib beside his blanket and stay there. Same loss. Different heart journey.

Or how he could watch a show or basketball game and not mentally hold the weight of our loss at the same time. Was he not distracted by the distraction? Was it not overstimulating for a nervous system that was just on high alert for so long? Same loss. Different heart journey.

By the end of most days, I feel the weight of everything. The tears. The business. A toddler who still needs me in all the ways toddlers do. Sometimes I could cry from sheer fatigue alone.

And then bedtime comes—stories to read, routines to keep, small hands to hold. And after that, I walk Carter's ashes back to his room. By the time I lay my head down, I have nothing left to give.

And the truth is...it feels unfair to Hugo.

I can feel myself at the edge—thin, worn, like one more demand might break me. And yet, I know he's tired too. He's carrying the same loss.

And in many ways, even more. Holding us together. Providing. Steadying what grief tries to shake.

And in the middle of all of this, there was a moment, quiet but piercing, when he looked at me and said, "Please don't forget about us."

Not demanding. Not frustrated. Just...honest.

That is a man giving everything he has and still reaching for the foundation of our home. And it stopped me. Because in the middle of losing one part of our family, we cannot lose each other too. The love between us—that is the reason Carter is part of our story at all.

So now, we are learning how to rebuild. It's not in grand gestures. It's not in some picture-perfect version of healing. But in small, daily choices that reflect a husband and wife trying their best to love through loss. Choosing to stay soft when it would be easier to shut down. Choosing to speak, even when it's messy. Choosing to reach for each other when grief would rather have us retreat inward. Some days, rebuilding looks like a conversation. Other days, it's just sitting next to each other in silence and not walking away.

We are not doing it perfectly. We are tired. We are changed in ways we are still trying to understand and allow ourselves to step into. Two different bodies. Two different grief responses. Trying to move as one.

This is what grief inside a marriage looks like. It is humanity colliding with eternity. And we are not always graceful. Personally, I stumble more than I stride. And some days, if I'm honest, it's a choice that doesn't come from strength. It comes from grace. The quiet, steady kind God provides, just enough for that day. Just enough to keep us from drifting too far apart. Not fixing the grief. But holding us inside it. And that's more than enough.

We choose—again and again—to show up. Together. Messy. Fragile…but not broken.

February 17, 2026

…it felt like we were just trying to get through the day without completely falling apart…I cling to every photo, every tangible item that draws me closer to Carter, and Hugo does not. I think it is just too incredibly painful.

In my mind, those things or moments held in time give Carter a presence…and in his mind they solidify his absence.

It's hard.

Navigating a living, breathing, marital love amidst tragedy is unbearable darkness you're just trying to survive—both without a map, and equally strained to remain standing.

Lately, I've limped my way through being a present wife and just pray he understands enough to give me grace and face another day, one more opportunity, to do better.

How do couples move through this—when the search for oneness gets repeatedly trampled by the burden of sorrow and all the pain it entails?

Another quiet morning. The silence is both peaceful and deafening.

CHAPTER 19
Two Sons

I've learned there are questions that used to be simple.

"Do you have children?"

Before Carter, the answer was easy. Clear. Contained. Now, it's the question that quietly splits me in two. My instinct is to say, "I have two boys." Because I do. But almost immediately, I feel the pressure to explain. To clarify and make it make sense for the person asking.

One here. One gone. One in my arms. One in eternity. And suddenly, what was true feels like it needs a footnote.

I've wrestled with that more than I expected. Am I not still the mother of two boys? Did death change the number of children I carry…or just where I carry them? Because I know what my body has held. I know the weight of both of them, and I know what it is to love two sons.

So why does it feel hard to just say it?

I think part of it is the moment that follows. The pause. The confusion. There's the question behind the question. It's the anticipation and weight of the sentence I have to say next: "My son passed away."

There is no net to gracefully catch that sentence. It lands heavy every time. So there's this quiet instinct to get ahead of it. To soften it. To manage the moment for them. But I'm learning something in this grief—My truth does not need to be edited to make it easier for someone else to understand.

I am a mother of two boys.

One I get to raise in front of me. One I carry in a way the world cannot see.

Both are mine, and both always will be. And maybe explanation isn't something I owe, but something I choose.

Chosen in safe spaces. Offered to those who can hold it.

But the truth itself? It stands on its own.

I am a mother of two boys.

April 1, 2026

There it is. April.

We enter the month he was supposed to come home. My heart can't believe it's here, but my heart is still hemorrhaging in January.

The air is warm. Spring is clearly here. Birds sing, flowers are blooming, trees awaken. It truly is the season for babies to arrive and hearts to be full.

I stared at his precious face a lot yesterday. I only have a handful of photos, but he is perfect in every way. We will be displaying a few at his service. I want people to see his face. To put a face to a name and a story. He's still my son.

Life moves forward at such a harsh pace, and I find myself clinging to his memory, his purpose, anything to remind the world of his existence.

My faith does not feel fragile, but my humanity does.

CHAPTER 20
Wrestling

There are moments my spirit rebels against my reality. Not from a place of shock. It's much deeper, less protective. Like something in me refuses to sign off on the truth that Carter is gone. That this is our story now. When I think, this isn't real... this can't be real. Like if I sit with it long enough, something will shift and I'll wake up from it.

But I don't.

It's often at night...I finish the last bedtime story. We sing "Away in a Manger" or "Silent Night"—usually both, because Beckham has never just wanted one.

I lay Beckham in his crib...and then gently carry Carter's ashes back to his crib across the hall. And that's when it hits. Breath in one crib. Remembrance in the other.

That inner tension—between what I know and what I feel—is exhausting. It feels like my soul is standing at a crossroads, caught between what I long for and what God has allowed.

David writes, "Why, my soul, are you downcast? Why so disturbed within me?" (Psalm 42:5 NIV). He isn't speaking from resolution—he's speaking into the unrest, calling his own heart back to truth.

And Jesus, in the garden—"O My Father, if it is possible, let this cup pass from Me" (Matthew 26:39 NKJV). The honest resistance. The plea for another way. And yet, "nevertheless not My will, but Yours, be done" (Luke 22:42 NKJV).

Two realities held at once. What He felt...and what He entrusted. That's what this feels like—and I imagine it's what many parents feel when losing a child. It's not the order of life and death. Not for a mother and her infant.

But even deeper than that, it presses on something at the very core of us: Death is the enemy. It is real—but it was never what God intended.

And it's tempting to believe that even entertaining these thoughts keeps me stuck...as if faithfulness means fully accepting what is, without wrestling.

But I'm reminded faith isn't the absence of tension.

It's standing at that crossroads—and choosing, sometimes with trembling hands, to trust God there. It's humanity getting a taste of both the deep sorrow of the flesh and the closeness of eternity.

I trust, not because it feels resolved. Not because my heart has caught up. But because He is still God in both places. Because the part of me that fights this reality is the same part of me that loves Carter so deeply.

And maybe faith isn't found in clean acceptance...but in bringing that conflicted, resisting heart to God—and staying.

Hallelujah even here.

March 22, 2026

Yesterday I sat looking over the menu from the catering company. Cucumber cups, fresh fruit, ughhh—why am I even here deciding what to feed people at my child's funeral?

Decisions often feel painfully hard to make, and yet not because they are major decisions. It's because deep down in my core, I do not want to be making them.

…there remains moments when my spirit, my bones, my heart, reject the fact that Carter is gone. That somehow, this is not my life, and it is a horrible nightmare.

Why do I even exhaust myself by thinking for one second it could be otherwise? Where is total acceptance of this reality? Does longing for something not to be true simply delay our faithfulness in moving forward? Am I wrong?

Most nights I just fall apart.

I have given all I can to mother, to love, to show up, and I just sit on the side of the bed and cry. Not a loud cry.

Not weeping. It's like the tears have been pressed from the depths of my soul and they come with exhaustive effort.

They are from the bottom of the hollow, and all I have left to give. Tears. That's it.

They are from the end of myself, and perhaps that is the beginning of acceptance…surrender.

CHAPTER 21
Good Friday

We lost our son. And it has undone me. There is nothing in me that would willingly choose that kind of suffering. There is nothing in me that would raise my hand and say, "Take mine… if it means someone else can live."

I wouldn't. And yet—this is the story of God.

He did not lose His Son by accident. He gave Him. On purpose. With full knowledge of the cost and full awareness of the suffering that would follow—betrayal, beating, the weight of sin He would carry. The kind of death you instinctually turn your face away from.

And still—He chose it.

Not for people who had it all together. Not for people who earned it. But for people like me. In my sin. In my doubt. In my anger. In the moments I question Him and wonder why my son is gone…He gave Jesus anyway.

I try to sit with that, and if I'm honest, it's hard to receive. Love like that feels almost too heavy. Too costly and too undeserved.

I know what it is to love a son…and lose a son. I know what it is to ache for him, to long for one more moment, one more breath, one more day. And knowing that, I cannot comprehend choosing to give him up.

But God did.

He watched it unfold and did not intervene. He did not stop the suffering. He did not pull Jesus down from the cross.

He stayed—through the suffering, the blood, the tears. He was there. Which means God is not distant from suffering. He is not unfamiliar with the ache of losing a child. He entered into it.

And somehow, in a way I am still wrestling to understand, His willingness to endure that kind of loss is the very thing that holds mine.

There's a heaviness that every Good Friday holds. It's especially heavy now. I find myself wanting to fast forward to Sunday. In a very real sense, yes—and also in the deepest hope of our faith.

I don't tie this up neatly. I don't have answers that make this easy.

Just this—The same God who did not spare His own Son… stayed.

Fully present. Fully God. Fully carrying the weight of Friday.

CHAPTER 22
Saturday

People say surrender like it's a decision. Like you wake up one day and choose to release it. But often during this season and especially today, this doesn't feel like a choice. It feels like I've simply run out of strength to hold it all.

And maybe…that's where surrender begins.

I remember reading from a father's experience after losing his daughter, and referring to the time from her death until they are reunited in Heaven as his Saturday. It's a nod to the Saturday after the crucifixion of Jesus. The day we rarely talk about… Friday was loud with suffering. Sunday would be loud with victory.

But Saturday—Saturday was quiet. Heavy. Uncertain. The in-between.

The place where everything looked finished…and nothing had been explained yet.

I understand his analogy with a clarity I never wanted, but feel in my bones. And the irony is not lost on me that as I write this, it is literally the Saturday after Good Friday.

So I sit in my own Saturday.

We can read Scripture now with the benefit of hindsight, knowing resurrection was only a day away. But the disciples and followers of Jesus didn't have that. All they had was loss, confusion, and silence.

And a God who, for a moment, felt very quiet.

That's what this space feels like. Not the moment of impact. Not the moment of redemption. Just…the space in between.

I still hold questions here. I still hold a story that does not make sense to me. And honestly, I still hold fear of the future.

Can I honor my son's existence and navigate the demands of life? Am I to mentally and emotionally prepare for another pregnancy? How do I hold that while still grieving the baby I just delivered…and lost?

What if we are unable to conceive? How do I hold that finality?

Saturday carries a weight all its own.

———————

I've built a life on discipline, on showing up, on doing what can be done. Control what you can control. Influence what you can influence. That's been tethered to my identity as long as I can remember.

But this, the space in between…this does not bend to discipline.

There is no amount of effort that can rewrite this story. No level of strength that can carry it cleanly. And so, something in me is loosening. Not because I want it to. But because it has to.

If this is surrender…it doesn't feel like peace.

It feels like open hands when I would rather be gripping tightly. It feels like releasing outcomes I never wanted to release. Letting go of timelines I had already written in my mind. And trusting a God I still have questions for.

But what has been very clear to me, is that surrender is not the absence of questions.

It's the willingness to stay…without answers.

So maybe that's what Saturday holds. Not clarity or resolution. Just trust. Trust that is often fragile and unpolished, but honest.

"God doesn't waste the wait."

I've heard that before, and I'm sure I've said it before. But here, in this space, it doesn't feel like something to explain. It feels like something to sit inside of.

The wait is not empty. It may be quiet, but it's not empty. Because if God was still at work on that first Saturday after His son's death, then I know He's at work after mine. I may not always see it or hear it, and the circumstance has not changed, but something is being held.

Not fixed. Not rushed.

Held.

If Friday is loss and Sunday is redemption, then Saturday is surrender. The place where I stop trying to carry what was never mine to carry alone. The place where I release the outcome—not because I'm ready, but because I can't hold it anymore.

I am in Saturday.

And if I'm honest, I don't know when Sunday will feel real.

But for now, this is where I am.

Open hands. Heavy heart. Learning, slowly, what it means to trust God in the in-between.

April 7, 2026

There are moments, very real ones, when I question all my writing. Hours of what feels like agony recalling events and navigating through the mud of emotions that I just go "for what?!"…I am not qualified in this. Whatever that means.

But then I think of Carter.

And I can't imagine his story, his purpose, losing its breath when he did. I genuinely believe God has greater plans through his tiny and brief life.

And while Carter recognized the voice and touch of his mommy, he also knows that of his Heavenly Father.

I can't imagine he misses me like I miss him. If there are no tears or sorrow in Heaven, then he cannot know my temporary absence. And that's more than okay. That's good.

I want my baby whole, happy, and held. Let me feel the tears. Let me feel the sorrow. Let me feel the longing.

Not my baby. Give him paradise.

I think about the day I held him, and now I realize that he steadied my breath and beat just as much as I steadied his.

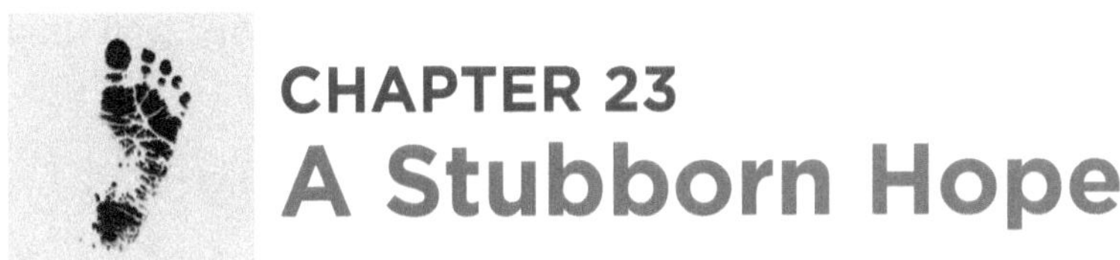

CHAPTER 23
A Stubborn Hope

There was a time when I thought hope would feel like relief. Like a lifting. Like the moment the weight finally shifts and you can breathe again.

But that's not true to my journey.

Hope, in this season, has not come in gently. It hasn't softened the ache or quieted the questions. It hasn't removed the reality that my son is gone.

If anything, it has met me right in the middle of it.

Not in the shock, when everything was blurred and my body was just trying to survive the impact. Not even in the early days of survival, when getting through an hour felt like enough.

But here. In the enduring.

This is where the reality has settled in. Where the silence is no longer shocking, just consistent. Where I wake up and remember…not because it just happened, but because it did. This is where I have come to know a different kind of hope.

Not the kind that carries you out. The kind that sits with you and refuses to leave. Stubborn.

I live in two realities now. One that I can touch—the empty space, the quiet moments, the absence that shows up in the most ordinary parts of my day. And one that I have to believe—that death is not the end, that my son is not lost, that what feels final here is not final forever.

Because of Christ, I know the grave is not the end of his story.

I know the cross was not just a moment in history, but a declaration—that death does not get the last word. And the truth is, they don't always feel like they fit together.

There are mornings I wake up and the first thought is still the same, *he's gone.*

Not figuratively. Not softened by language. Gone.

And no amount of truth about eternity changes the way that lands in my body. I still feel the weight of missing him. I still move through a life that keeps asking things of me—a toddler who needs me, a home to care for, responsibilities that don't pause for grief.

And I am tired.

Not the kind of tired that sleep fixes, but the kind that comes from carrying something invisible and heavy everywhere you go.

This is where the tension lives. Between what I know is true…and what I feel every single day.

And still…hope remains.

Not loud. Not triumphant. Not the kind that makes sense of any of this. It doesn't rush in with answers. It doesn't take the weight from my hands. It simply stays.

Stubborn. Steady. Unmoved by my exhaustion. Unafraid of my questions.

Hope that sits beside the grief and refuses to leave. Hope that doesn't ask me to feel strong, only to keep going. Hope that anchors itself somewhere deeper than my emotions can reach.

And I know where that hope comes from. Not from me. Not from my ability to stay strong or hold it together.

But from Christ.

From the One who stepped into death Himself and walked out of it. From the One who does not ask me to understand, but invites me to trust. From the One who holds my son in a place I cannot yet see.

I don't always feel Him. But He is there. He is our hope.

And He stays.

March 27, 2026

The fatigue at this point is different. It's no longer shock and survival. It's reliving and enduring.

I wake up and immediately pick up my reality—mothering a son here, in the present, and mothering a son in eternity.

Carry both. Love both. Mother both.

Figuring out how to mother your child in Heaven, honor him and his story, and remain true to a journey uniquely your own is a constant unfolding. There is no handbook or guidance. You're just thrown into an arena you never asked to be in, and now fighting for breath. Every breath.

There is no "right way," but I do find myself wanting some kind of validation, or dare I say, approval, that I am headed in a healthy direction—whatever that means.

I do know I want God near, constantly. Redirecting my thoughts to Him is the only way I feel like I can keep moving and keep my savior and son close.

The worst has already happened. The nightmare is my reality.

I find myself constantly standing at the end of that statement with the heaviest question: Now what?...and no clear answer.

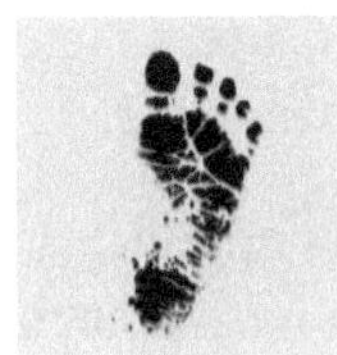

CHAPTER 24
Coming Up for Air

There is a fear, especially after death brushes so close, that joy is a betrayal. That laughter somehow dishonors the weight of what happened. That if you aren't immersed in sorrow at all times, you're forgetting.

And truth is, there is a twinge of guilt. It may be subtle. But it surfaces.

It tends to show up the first time you realize you can still function. When you answer emails, make decisions, handle business, laugh briefly, or even just feel steady for a few hours.

Something inside says, "How can I do this when my child is gone?"

Sometimes it's small. Beckham laughing across the room. Feeling accomplished after three loads of laundry and a batch of muffins. A moment where Hugo and I look at each other and realize we just laughed without thinking.

And then it hits me—Carter should be here too.

For a split second the betrayal flickers. How can this moment exist when he isn't in it?

But that's not how love works.

Those moments are a reminder that love is the root of our sorrow, and love still exists in other forms around us. The heart that aches for Carter is the very heart that delights in Beckham's voice or lingers in a shared look with my husband. Carter's mere existence awakened our hearts in ways we'd never imagine.

The joy doesn't cancel the grief. The exhale does not dismiss the tears that fell the night before. They exist alongside each other. Praise God, they are mercies.

When laughter comes, it is not comic relief. It is fresh oxygen to lungs that have been running on adrenaline and fear for too long. It is grace entering a body that has carried too much.

The grief is deep. It is sacred. It is real. But it is not total immersion. It is not the only current running through our home.

Joy exists. Mercy shows up. Smiles occur. Laughter captures us.

These moments matter. They mean death has not swallowed our capacity for life.

We hold the grief. We walk through it. But we are not living inside it. Death occurred, but breath continues.

And that breath is a gift from a good God who has not abandoned us in the valley.

Those small flashes of joy are reminders that goodness still threads through our days. That God is strong enough to carry our heartache while still placing beauty in front of us—joy that is uncomplicated and not naïve to its cost.

The fact that those moments exist, even in the minority, is beautiful. They allow you and me to come up for air and often where God quietly steadies our feet so the grief doesn't swallow us whole.

I'm relearning every day that grief and joy are not opposites. Through Christ, they are companions—walking beside each other until the day grief disappears and only joy remains.

Loss changes you permanently. But that doesn't require you to stop living.

In Scripture there's a quiet pattern in suffering: God does not require constant collapse to prove love or grief.

Even in the Psalms of lament, David moves between despair and steadiness in the same breath.

"I am weary with my groaning…" (Psalm 6:6 NKJV)

…and then a few lines later…

"But the Lord has heard my cry for mercy" (Psalm 6:9 NIV).

Grief hits in waves. Mercy is the air between them.

And I cling to these reminders. They are the exact moments where God carries. Loves. Steadies. Joy does not mean the grief is fading. It means God is sustaining…That breath is mercy and love remains.

CHAPTER 25
What Remains

I think we often talk about refinement like it's gentle. Like something soft. Intentional. Almost peaceful. Like God slowly shaping something beautiful while everything else in life continues as normal.

That has not been my experience.

Refining, at least here, feels more like being stripped than being polished.

It's the quiet removal of things that once felt important. The dulling of urgency toward things that used to drive me. The inability to care about what once consumed my thoughts. It's not dramatic. It's not loud. It's not even always emotional.

It's quiet. Almost uncomfortably quiet.

I noticed the shift first in my senses. I no longer wanted to be around loud people or crowded spaces. What once felt normal now felt overwhelming—like pouring kerosene on a nervous system that had been on high alert for too long.

Noise didn't just feel loud. It felt intrusive. Violent on my soul.

My body started craving quiet in a way I couldn't ignore. Not as a preference, but as a necessity.

I also noticed the shift in my identity.

For so long, I had it tightly wound around productivity. What I could get done. What I could move forward. What I could check off.

There was a rhythm to it that felt satisfying, at least on the surface. But if I'm honest, it was a kind of satisfaction that only came at the end. Completion felt good. But the process often felt…empty.

Now, I feel that grip loosening. Not in a way that makes me careless—but in a way that feels more honest. I would not have chosen the circumstances to get here or gain perspective, but God knows that too.

I'm not as driven by an endless to-do list that demands to be finished in order to feel enough. I'm starting to be moved by something quieter—Purpose.

Not the kind that shouts or strives. It's the kind that steadies. The kind that doesn't need constant proof—just faithfulness in what's in front of me.

My days are simple right now.

I wake up early, before the house stirs, because I need the stillness. There is something about quiet that feels like oxygen in this season. I need to sit, to breathe, to pray, to ground my feet and my soul.

Then it's the rhythm of the day: our toddler's needs, laundry, meals, keeping a home running, business demands, writing when I can, responding to a few people who feel safe.

On paper, it could look small. Maybe even uneventful in some aspects. But it doesn't feel hollow. It feels necessary and purposeful.

There was a time when I would have questioned this pace. Truth be told, I would have rebelled at the very thought of it. Wondered if I was doing enough, producing enough, moving forward enough. Now those questions feel distant.

Not because I've figured something out—but because something in me has been reordered and my capacity recalibrated to the necessary pace, not the chosen.

When you've held both life and death in the same breath, a lot of the urgency that once defined your days doesn't carry the same weight. And for a while, that shift can feel disorienting. Like standing in a room where all the furniture has been removed. You know something is happening.

But you're not sure what fills the space yet. Nothingness. Still, with a purpose.

I think that's where refining is often misunderstood. We expect it to feel like clarity. But sometimes it feels like absence.

We expect it to come with direction. But sometimes it comes with stillness.

We expect it to build something new immediately. But often, it starts by quietly dismantling what was. Expectations, dreams, plans, all swept up in the aftermath of loss.

Dismantled.

This season isn't about becoming more. It's about becoming true. And honestly, that process is slower than I would have chosen. Quieter than I would have imagined. And at times, more uncomfortable than I know how to explain.

There are moments where I catch myself wondering, Now what?

Not in a panicked way. More like a steady question that sits in the background of my days. Because when so much gets placed into the category of doesn't matter, you're left holding what does. And sometimes…that list feels very small.

But maybe that's the point.

Maybe refinement isn't about expanding your life. Maybe it's about reducing it down to what can actually carry the weight of it.

Right now, I know a few things do. My faith. My husband. And this pull to write—to put words to what has been lived, in hopes that someone else walking through this kind of valley doesn't feel as alone.

That feels real. And for now, that is enough.

This version of me moves differently. Slower. More intentionally.

Less concerned with how much gets done, and more aware of what actually carries weight.

And while part of me still feels the tension of that shift… another part of me knows this isn't lost. It's something being made true.

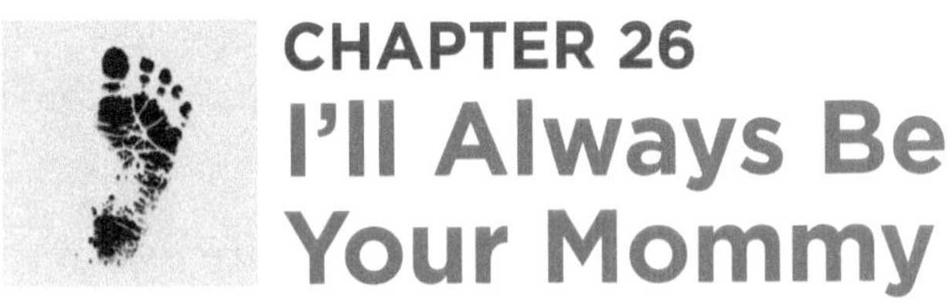

CHAPTER 26
I'll Always Be Your Mommy

I am still learning how to carry the loss of Carter every day.

Some mornings feel steady. Others feel like I'm picking it up all over again.

There are quiet moments when I sit in his room, holding the small bag of his ashes in my hands. It's hardly a handful.

I don't always know what to say. Most of the time, I don't say much at all. But almost every time, without thinking, I find myself whispering, "I'll always be your mommy."

I don't fully know why that's what comes out.

Maybe it's instinct. Maybe it's truth my heart is trying to hold onto. Or maybe it's the only way I know how to keep loving him in a place I cannot reach.

"I'll always be your mommy."

Not past tense. Not something that ended. Something that continues.

I think about Mary sometimes. After Jesus died...and then rose...and then ascended into Heaven. She knew who He was. She knew there was purpose, and she knew the story didn't end in death. And still, He was her son.

I have to believe there was an ache there.

A longing that didn't disappear just because heaven was real. A love that didn't become less earthly just because it became eternal.

Maybe she held both too. The truth of who He was…and the reality that she could no longer hold Him.

I understand something now that I didn't before—that a mother can know God's goodness, trust His plan, believe in eternity…and still long for her child.

I still crave a quiet start—the kind that lets me ground myself before the world gets loud. Prayer. Scripture. Journaling. Sitting long enough to feel what is actually there. The tears still come.

But not always from the same place.

Sometimes they come from the sharpness of missing him. Sometimes from the weight of what could have been. And sometimes, unexpectedly, from a place of steady gratitude—as though I was trusted to love him at all.

I've changed in what I care about.

I care far less about how I'm perceived, and far more about whether I am living in the purpose God has placed in front of me.

There's a clarity now that I didn't have before. A stripping away of what doesn't matter.

And yet, I find myself softer toward people. More aware that everyone is carrying something. That most people are wading through waters I may know nothing about. I try to meet people there, without assumption, without needing to fully understand. Compassion.

I also no longer feel the need to make people comfortable in my grief. That has been growth.

I don't rush to soften it. I don't reach for words that make it easier to hear. I've learned that discomfort is not something to fix—it's something people have to decide to step into. And when they do, when they choose to sit in the valley with me, I exhale. I'm grateful for the willingness and courage.

There have been people who have done exactly that. Who didn't look away. Who didn't try to tidy up what cannot be tidied. And it has changed me.

They inspire me to stay. To sit. To not rush someone out of their sorrow. They are doing holy work without knowing it.

I think about eternity differently now.

We speak of Heaven in ways that can feel distant, almost abstract. A place we believe in, but don't quite see. Streets of gold, no tears, no suffering, constant worship.

But when your child is there…it is no longer abstract. It is personal.

I don't think I have ever longed for eternity the way I do now. Not out of escape, but out of connection. My precious Carter is on the other side of it.

And so I find myself living in two places at once. Loving and mothering on both sides of eternity.

Holding Beckham in my arms, fully here, fully present—while also holding Carter in my heart, in a way that is just as real, just as constant.

And maybe that's what that whisper is. "I'll always be your mommy."

Something that continues, just in a different place.

I am learning not to rush either. Not to rush past the joy in front of me nor past the sorrow behind me.

They exist together, hand in hand. Brothers.

There is joy now. Real joy. And there is still pain. Deep, unrelenting at times. Both live here. And I see more clearly because of it. Not just in what matters, but in the stark contrast of who I was before Carter, and who I am now.

And so I find myself here—not at the end of his story, but in the middle of one I cannot fully see and yet fully trust.

Our baby lived.

He is with Jesus.

And I am still his mommy.

Hallelujah even here.

About The Author

Our beautiful family while pregnant with Carter, December 2025

Meredith Nolasco is a faith-based writer, entrepreneur, and co-owner of Elite Human Performance, where she has spent more than two decades helping individuals pursue lasting strength in body, mind, and lifestyle. A graduate of Elon University, Meredith's professional background in coaching has shaped her ability to connect deeply with people, guiding them through both physical and personal transformation.

Her journey into writing grew organically from years of journaling, reflection, and creating fitness and wellness content. Over time, her voice expanded into the Christian nonfiction and inspirational memoir space, where she explores themes such as faith, grief, resilience, and motherhood. Known for her honest and reflective style, Meredith writes with emotional clarity and spiritual depth, offering readers a space that feels both personal and grounded in truth.

A defining influence on her work is the loss of her son, Carter, an experience that reshaped her understanding of trust, suffering, and God's presence in life's most difficult moments. Rather than offering simple answers, Meredith's writing meets readers in the tension of real life, speaking to those navigating grief, loss, and questions of purpose. Her message centers on the belief that every story holds meaning and that faith can remain steady even when circumstances are not.

Meredith's mission as an author is to foster connection, encourage authenticity, and remind others they are not alone in their journey. She is passionate about helping readers engage their own stories with courage, honesty, and hope.

She lives in North Carolina with her husband, Hugo, and their son, Beckham, where she continues to write, coach, and invest in the rhythms of everyday life that shape her perspective and message.

Connect with Meredith at:

Meredith.hallelujahevenhere@gmail.com